Yesterday, Today, Tomorrow

and all the flowers in-between

Ralyn Siegh

BookLeaf Publishing
India | USA | UK

Made with ❤ on the BookLeaf Publishing Platform
www.bookleafpub.in
www.bookleafpub.com

Dedication

To my Mom, Brother and Sister.

I love you all <3

Preface

My Nana's house was absolutely surrounded by flowers. Most women in my family boast beautiful gardens, or had, but this is about one in particular. In her backyard, Nana had a rather large bush of Yesterday, Today, and Tomorrow. Like her, I fell in love with the multicolor flowers, and curiously inspected the plant every chance I got. That task became demanding, once my family moved in for her care. Something that had drastically shifted our dynamic, but a choice I am infinitely grateful for now.

In one way I'm indebted to Nana is by her mother. Had we not been in close company, I'm not sure if I would be so knowledgeable of my Great-Great Grandma. She was a poet. Moreso, the very first poet that would inspire this passion in me. In these poems, I hope to share a piece of me with you, as she had with me, and inspire life and the love of it, as her story will always provide.

Acknowledgements

Shout-out to the greatest inspirations I'm not related to: God; Victorian Flower language, and various sources; Authors like Lewis Caroll, Holly Black, and Victoria Aveyard; English Teachers Miss Bieber, Mrs. Williamson, and Miss Greene; Musicians (my saving grace) Sleep Token, Sophie Hunter, and VeggieTales; Celsius.

1. Lilacs

Oh, how very often
Do I think on Spring.

Remembering sweet April,
Devoted to purity.

Renewing through phases,
Rebirth with Spirituality.

Finally, that anodyne fragrance
Leads me to calming pastel.

Bright clusters that soothe,
Refreshing nostalgia, as well.

Frozen in time, or Déjà vu,
I ever retreat to April.

2. Marigold

She quietly watches,
Clutching an blossom, auspicious,
Close to her chest.

This strength she found,
Power from the Sun,
Could shine light all around.

But she'd turn on her heel,
Hide behind a smile,
Find despair through peculiar trial.

Down every path she'd lead,
It trailed behind a row of seed,
That give bloom to resilience she'd need.

Caged between her palms,
The little bud grows, warms,
To ignite joy against her qualms.

3. Carnations

When she was young,
Fascinated by pinks and yellows,
She would look to butterflies,
For comfort in sorrows.

And as she bloomed,
Cutting weakness away for renewal,
She called herself Dianthus,
Encouraged by distinction.

Then, at a loss for words,
Met with disappointment,
She feared only rejection,
Insecurity's pompous incarnation.

4. Daisies

Craft a crown out of patience and purity.

Inflorescence that whisper of life's divinity.

Day's bright children of cheerful countenance.

Promise opens hope to innocence.

Chains bound in secret and simplicity.

Objectified, no love found in sympathy.

Preserve clarity as perfectly pressed.

Search new beginnings in life's promise.

5. Sunflowers

Every summer, I follow the same
Aesthetics, commitments only in name:

Unrequited passions, dreams of happiness,
Calls for loyalty and confidence.

Adoration in fashion of Clytie to Apollo;
Rising and falling, after the sun I follow.

6. Forget-Me-Not

Walk on in remembrance,
Keep this humble promise,
Wander through a forest,
Daunting and dense at blue hour.

Faithfulness and fidelity
Were strangers to me,
Of course my steps would founder.

Before I fall,
Forget me not! I call
Out to love that's true.

7. Chrysanthemum

Yesterday was only a moment, say,
Autumn, for memory's season.

As it passes I could stay,
But, I choose to linger as if
I were a stubborn flower, mid-November,
Something delicate, daisy-like nature;
A sign for cheerfulness, however miniature.

Though that every lamentation, any
Death, failure through adversity
Passing by with every day before
Should look again--

Bright as gold--

Among an array of decorative beds
To see the blessed promise of growth.

Look again on Yesterday, and find
This solitary bud, sown from an oath:
Small things will become great,
You can leave old things behind.

8. Bluebell

Head hung low in humility,
With gratitude and honesty,
She beseeches Memory:

Recall, but not in constancy.
For Innocence's sake, offer serenity;
Understanding, provide through the in-between.

That she can move on with tranquility,
Through woodlands, she summons love everlasting.
Magic in the kindness of lowly things.

9. Camellia

Beloved,

Reflect on the depths of you.
A fountain of unconditional love,
Channeled through the deepest truths.
You are bright, know your spirit is bold;
Adoring, devoted to empathy,
You hold wisdom in your soul.
Persistence and strength, your beauty;
Affirm your intuition in peace.

10. Poppy

Surely, I am the grass crowding refuge,
Surrounding entirely the sleepy red flowers.

Seeking consolation for set-tos,
Strength and perseverance of a wildflower.

Struggles and sacrifice nourish Insomnia,
Supplicate peace eternal's rest.

Sleeping flowers fading dim and blah,
Single blades bowing faithfully in remembrance.

Surely, I am withering, leadened,
Still, I find veneration in Death's garden.

11. Zinnia

Some days will call for your absence;
Most days fail to fulfill your needs;
Each day's a token of endurance.

You'll greet Today, ambitions unaltered:
Do your best, do your part.
Hard work pays off to steadfastness, don't falter.

12. Hyacinths

Along the way, she makes acquaintance
With sisters, Hyacinths. Each blossom's beauty
Committed intentions.
Twin skirts painted red,
Twirl relaxed in the wind. Lighthearted whimsy
Demands kind compliment!
Such joy you inspire, she calls to one below.
Tickled pink, she twists out with adagio;
Meanwhile, dear sister turns yellow.
And of me? What do you admire? The flower
Inquires with exigency; however,
Takes no account of her companion's apparel.
In one blossom's ire, the other's bloom pales white--
Pure flower wishing deeply for respite--
Finally taking notice, yellow perses at the sight.
Sister, forgiveness is all I desire, the flower continues,
Pleads sincere to her selfsame; skirts adorned blue.
Hardly one for emnity, she replies with her ardor, *I bear no malice to you!*
The sisters giggle and embrace, blushing in delight.
Then carry on their intended way, without so much a goodbye.

13. Daffodil

Today, she's December,
Herald to inspiration, rebirth.

Conspicuous youthfulness,
Vitality in daily inner death.

Today, she is Myth,
Alluring to Fancy's whim.

Intoxicated by her muse,
Lycorine, creativity is abused.

Today, she's Awareness,
Enchanted like Narcissus.

In her reflection, clarity,
Forgiveness the only remedy.

14. Anemone

In bad luck and omens, she's never forsaken.

The windflowers bloomed in anticipation.

Their delicate petals ensuring protection.

Fragility transient to rain, winking a promise of leisure again.

15. Aster

The first step is careful,
Anxious she'll fall.

Yet keeping her pace, she'll find,
Although she's been patient, she's falling behind.

Have faith and show valor,
Stoke courage, little star.

Tomorrow's not promised;
Be confident in what you've done so far.

16. Iris

I have something to tell you,
She whispers, a hurried exchange,
A message for hope, positivity, too:
Have faith you will accept change.

17. Snapdragons

As you go on your course,
Beware this obstacle's curse.
It stops all who wander with preternatural force.

Old advice, your future's protection:
Hold onto graciousness and strength.
This beast relies on deception.

Dual nature, her only restraint--
Don't surrender to deviousness,
Refuse her endearments.

Avoid mystery concealed under the surface;
Instead, offer her only detachment.
She cannot poison your purpose.

18. Violet

Anger and pride,
Her personal nuance,
Suffering only inside.

Humility, modesty her penance
For ambition only in vanity.
But, Wisdom whispers in confidence:

You are neither mouse nor bird but, royalty.
Devote your imagination to faithfulness,
Your reward is my loyalty.

19. Lotus

Rise up out of hiding, be resilient,
This is not your end.

Your calling is higher,
This transformation your rebirth.

20. Lilies

Above all else,
Weigh virtue in these:
Innocence in heart, and
Purity in soul.

Burdened in transience,
A lesson against presentiment
From the generations precedent,
Opens us to beauty is life's cycle

21. Peonies

Put away timidness, bashfulness, and shame.
This life is yours,
There's no room for Superstition's game.

Romance and beauty she'll promise, sure.
But, honor and ideals are always dependable,
In the case of Tomorrow.

Take heart after Paeon,
When influence is hardly reputable,
Seek knowledge before good fortune.

www.ingramcontent.com/pod-product-compliance
Lightning Source LLC
Chambersburg PA
CBHW062111140826
49812CB00058B/1251
9789370921764